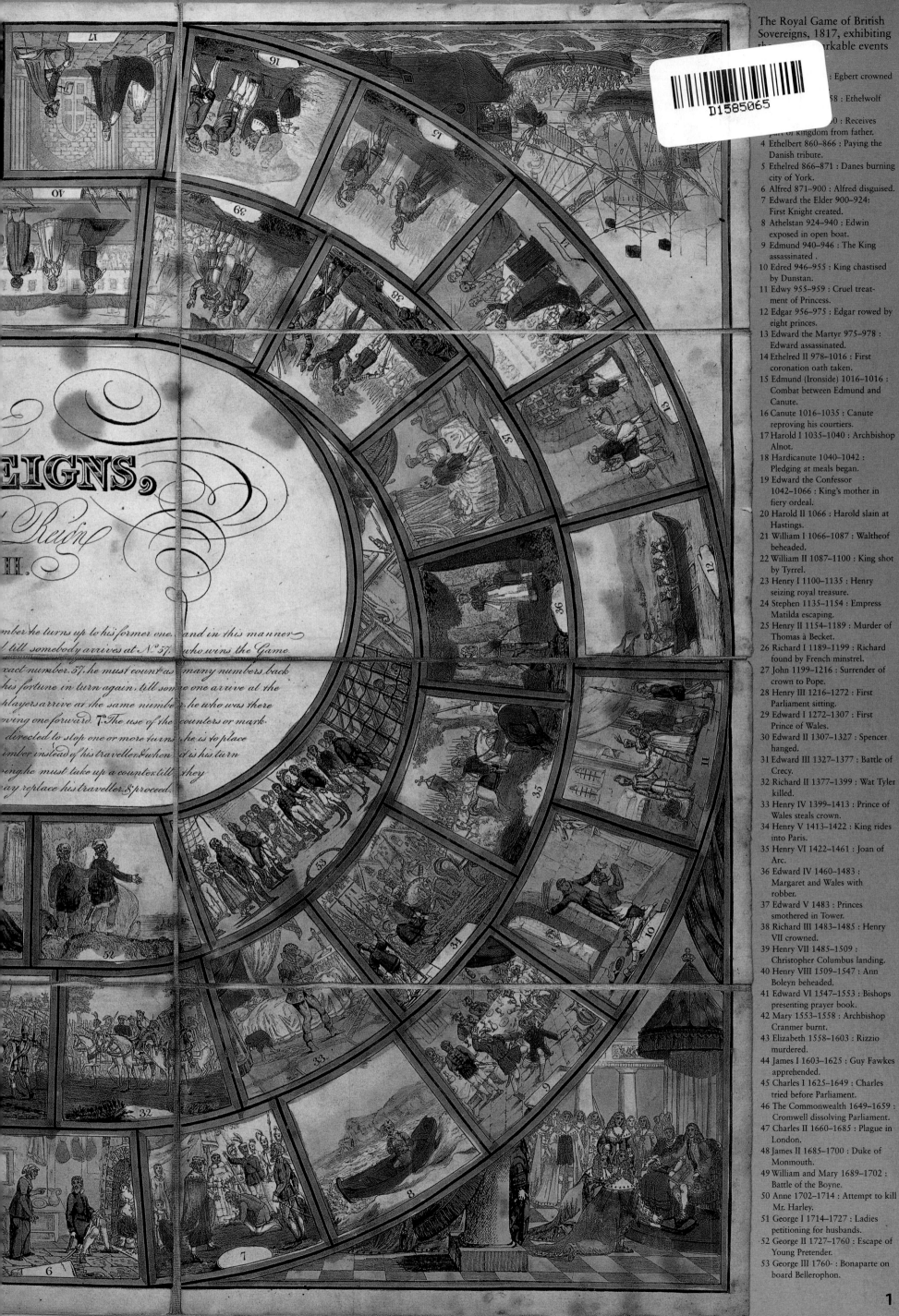

The Royal Game of British Sovereigns, 1817, exhibiting the [most] remarkable events [of each reign].

1 [Egbert 827–838] : Egbert crowned [...]
2 [Ethelwolf 838–8]58 : Ethelwolf [...]
3 [...8]0 : Receives part of kingdom from father.
4 Ethelbert 860–866 : Paying the Danish tribute.
5 Ethelred 866–871 : Danes burning city of York.
6 Alfred 871–900 : Alfred disguised.
7 Edward the Elder 900–924: First Knight created.
8 Athelstan 924–940 : Edwin exposed in open boat.
9 Edmund 940–946 : The King assassinated .
10 Edred 946–955 : King chastised by Dunstan.
11 Edwy 955–959 : Cruel treatment of Princess.
12 Edgar 956–975 : Edgar rowed by eight princes.
13 Edward the Martyr 975–978 : Edward assassinated.
14 Ethelred II 978–1016 : First coronation oath taken.
15 Edmund (Ironside) 1016–1016 : Combat between Edmund and Canute.
16 Canute 1016–1035 : Canute reproving his courtiers.
17 Harold I 1035–1040 : Archbishop Alnot.
18 Hardicanute 1040–1042 : Pledging at meals began.
19 Edward the Confessor 1042–1066 : King's mother in fiery ordeal.
20 Harold II 1066 : Harold slain at Hastings.
21 William I 1066–1087 : Waltheof beheaded.
22 William II 1087–1100 : King shot by Tyrrel.
23 Henry I 1100–1135 : Henry seizing royal treasure.
24 Stephen 1135–1154 : Empress Matilda escaping.
25 Henry II 1154–1189 : Murder of Thomas à Becket.
26 Richard I 1189–1199 : Richard found by French minstrel.
27 John 1199–1216 : Surrender of crown to Pope.
28 Henry III 1216–1272 : First Parliament sitting.
29 Edward I 1272–1307 : First Prince of Wales.
30 Edward II 1307–1327 : Spencer hanged.
31 Edward III 1327–1377 : Battle of Crecy.
32 Richard II 1377–1399 : Wat Tyler killed.
33 Henry IV 1399–1413 : Prince of Wales steals crown.
34 Henry V 1413–1422 : King rides into Paris.
35 Henry VI 1422–1461 : Joan of Arc.
36 Edward IV 1460–1483 : Margaret and Wales with robber.
37 Edward V 1483 : Princes smothered in Tower.
38 Richard III 1483–1485 : Henry VII crowned.
39 Henry VII 1485–1509 : Christopher Columbus landing.
40 Henry VIII 1509–1547 : Ann Boleyn beheaded.
41 Edward VI 1547–1553 : Bishops presenting prayer book.
42 Mary 1553–1558 : Archbishop Cranmer burnt.
43 Elizabeth 1558–1603 : Rizzio murdered.
44 James I 1603–1625 : Guy Fawkes apprehended.
45 Charles I 1625–1649 : Charles tried before Parliament.
46 The Commonwealth 1649–1659 : Cromwell dissolving Parliament.
47 Charles II 1660–1685 : Plague in London.
48 James II 1685–1700 : Duke of Monmouth.
49 William and Mary 1689–1702 : Battle of the Boyne.
50 Anne 1702–1714 : Attempt to kill Mr. Harley.
51 George I 1714–1727 : Ladies petitioning for husbands.
52 George II 1727–1760 : Escape of Young Pretender.
53 George III 1760– : Bonaparte on board Bellerophon.

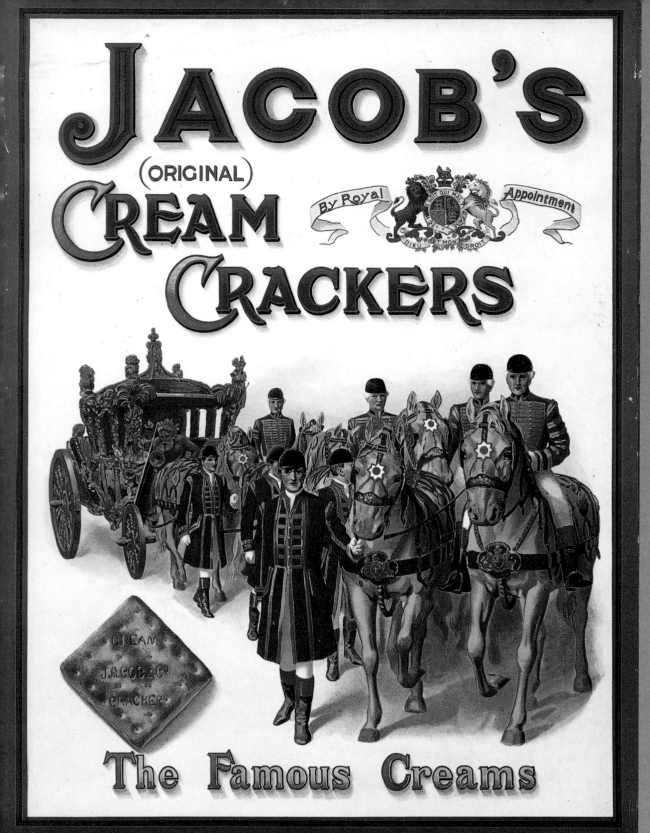

JACOB'S (ORIGINAL) CREAM CRACKERS

By Royal Appointment

The Famous Creams

Jacob's cream crackers advertisement, 1911.

The state coach was built in 1762 for George III. It was designed by Sir William Chambers with paintings by Cipriani; the total weight came to four tons and the cost was £7,661-17s-5d.

Contents

Royal Souvenirs

The number and diversity of royal souvenirs has been immense, ranging from expensive limited edition ceramics to mass-produced flags and throwaway paper bags. The 1,500 examples in this book are but a selection of many thousands that have existed. Such mementoes serve as a reminder of a particular occasion, but also capture the family memory caught up with that moment. Those souvenirs from earlier times become evocative of an age in which our parents or grandparents once lived. And yet centuries ago, long before the arrival of television and the popular press, the royal mug or plaque served as a way of getting the royal image into people's homes and was originally a symbol of support and loyalty to a particular sovereign.

Amongst the royal souvenirs below is a paper napkin for the opening of Tower Bridge in 1894, a tin containing 'best mixed pins' from 1902, a small Fry's chocolate box and a Cadbury's bookmark of 1911, a 1935 silver jubilee poster designed by Fawkes for display in the London Underground, a Burdall's paper bag and a tin for Edward VIII's coronation (a removable lapel badge has been embodied into the design of the lid). A red, white and blue condom was available in 1937 – what remains is shown below (front centre). From the 1953 coronation there is a powder compact (two more examples are on the back cover), a tea towel, a plastic puzzle, and a Daintee confectionery tin with an informal photograph of the Queen and Duke.

The coming of the photographic age enabled both an accurate likeness of and intimacy with royalty, which encouraged a far greater interest in their lives. Queen Victoria had been photographed first in 1857. Photographs enlivened newspapers and magazines, making them the most widely distributed of all royal souvenirs, not just at royal occasions, but also at times of intrigue. One such instance was when Princess Margaret fell in love with Group Captain Peter Townsend, a romance which lasted many years, but ended in 1955 with the *Daily Express* headline (below). There have been hundreds of photographs of the royal family on the balcony of Buckingham Palace – few commoners have joined them, one exception being Winston Churchill celebrating victory in 1945.

Introduction

The first commemorative item for a coronation was a medal struck for Edward VI, and cast in gold or silver; the inscription ended, "crowned 19 February 1547 at the age of ten years". Medals continued to be made thereafter for each monarch. Other types of souvenir were available during the 17th century, such as glass goblets and pottery plates and mugs. For instance, for Charles II's accession in 1660 there were Delft wine cups on sale illustrated with a half-length portrait of the king in ceremonial robes.

The royal lineage has often been unpredictable and sometimes there was more than one claim to the throne. Such was the case when James II's popularity waned and he fled when confronted by an army raised by Prince William of Orange who had sailed from Holland in 1688. William's wife was James II's eldest daughter. William and Mary were crowned as joint king and queen of England in 1689 – loyal subjects could have purchased a Dutch Delft plaque (such as on the right) to show their allegiance. Even by the early nineteenth century, pottery souvenirs were still expensive; paper was becoming cheaper. The announcement of George IV's coronation in 1821 along with local celebrations of that day were recorded on this economical four by five inch piece of paper.

It was while Oliver Cromwell was defeating royalist troops in England that Charles II was crowned king of England, Scotland and Ireland at Scoone in Scotland on 1 January 1651. This ceremony was documented in a publication (above) which was then secretly reprinted in London and distributed to royalist supporters as evidence that the coronation had actually taken place. The service was described in 38 pages, of which 23 recorded a tedious sermon. After an impressive feast, the new king played a round of golf. Charles II restored the monarchy to England in 1660.

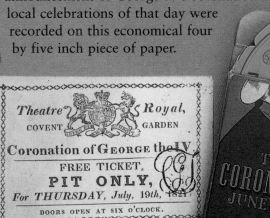

Whether through loyalty, curiosity or just the need to watch an historic event, crowds have always gathered to see a royal procession. Only the privileged could be accommodated inside Westminster Abbey. For the coronation of George IV in 1821, a re-enactment of the occasion was shown at the Theatre Royal in the evening of the same day and continued to be performed for many weeks.

Since then, illustrations, photographs, cinema newsreels, radio, cine film and finally television have brought royal scenes to the masses – better than being stuck behind a fat lady.

It was the dignitaries of towns and cities who ensured that school children had mementoes of royal events, whether souvenir mugs or chocolates in a commemorative tin. The mayor's name would often be added to the mug or tin. A 'ticket to tea' (above) would be another treat. Manufacturers also aligned themselves with royalty, as with this certificate of merit, c.1911.

For the coronation of William IV and Adelaide in 1830, there were not only mugs, but also a coronation dissected puzzle (later known as a jigsaw), with its hand-coloured guide and a box. The same design, with a change of sovereign, was used in 1838 (see p.10).

I saw a fat lot at the last Coronation.

The earliest souvenir tins were made from a base metal, although that for Queen Caroline (c.1820) had an inset brass lid. Later examples were filled with brass and steel paste.

"Presented gratis with the Atlas newspaper", this highly embossed card (left) of George III, c.1820, was a refined gift. The engraved card (above) of Adelaide and William IV was a prestigious gift for Jennings the hatter to hand to his customers in 1830.

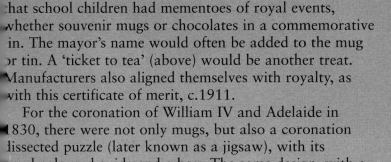

'Dissected maps for teaching geography' were first devised as an educational aid in the 1760s. Wallis's 'Royal chronological tables of English history' was published in 1788, and was used to teach children history; each section contained the remarkable events and eminent persons of the particular reign.

Royal history

The traditional way of connecting children with British history has been through the progression of ruling kings and queens. For those who could afford them, the dissected puzzle or jigsaw (as they became known after the introduction of the mechanical fretsaw in the 1870s) was one way of making history more interesting. The examples above date from Wallis's chronological tables of 1788 to those from early in Queen Victoria's reign. The small card (left) of the 'History and correct likeness of the British sovereigns, from William the Conqueror to Victoria the First' did not contain the dates of each monarch's reign. Board games (below) were another way in which history could be fun, enjoyed by both young and old.

Board games began to be published in the 1750s, often using a geographical subject such as 'A Journey through Europe'(1759). Another popular game was that based on an historical theme, an early example being 'Royal Genealogical Pastime of the Sovereigns' (c.1838), 'Historical Pastime' or 'a new game of the History of England from the Conquest to the Accession of George the Third' (1803), and an updated version of 1828 where George IV's image was in the centre and the last circle of the game track recorded the death of Queen Caroline in 1821. At the front of this book is reproduced the 'Royal Game of British Sovereigns', 'exhibiting the most remarkable events in each reign from Egbert to Geo II'. It was published by J. & E. Wallis in 1817.

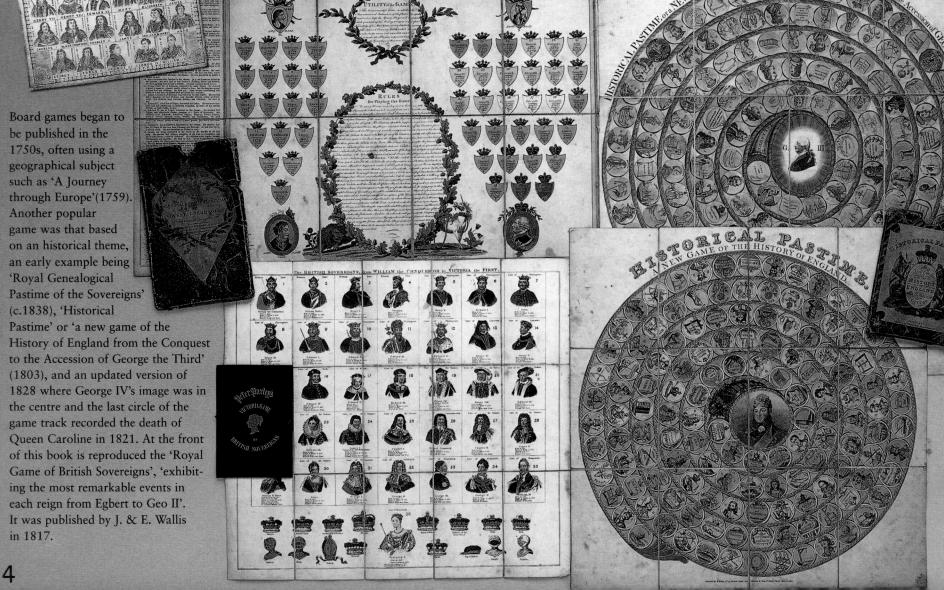

In the Public Eye

For hundreds of years, the monarch had lived aloof from his subjects, ruling in a more or less autocratic manner. However, by the 1640s a constitutional struggle had developed between parliament and King Charles I, which turned into an armed conflict. Found guilty of treason, Charles was beheaded in 1649.

With the development of printing and the arrival of journals and newspapers in the seventeenth century, news and opinions travelled further and faster. The isolation of the monarchy was no more; the public gaze focused on their abilities and weaknesses, but it was their frailties that were more often discussed.

In today's television-hungry world with the prying camera lens, it is difficult for royalty not to be in the public eye. Indeed, there have been times when the medium of television has helped, as in ITV's 'A Much Maligned Monarch' with Prince Charles in 1976, or BBC's nine-part series 'Royal Heritage' in 1977, or the informal 'It's a Knockout' in 1987 with Anne, Edward, Andrew and Fergie.

The sovereign's face appears on postage stamps, coins and banknotes, and ships, hospitals, pubs and waterfalls are named after royalty. Constantly in the public mind, there is no getting away from them; whether in Eastenders' Albert Square and Queen Vic or in Coronation Street, the monarch is inextricably linked with our society.

The golden age of visual satire was during the 1790s and the early years of the nineteenth century. Political cartoon drawing with hand-coloured embellishments opened the eyes of British society in an image-starved era. James Gillray depicted the mighty King George III confronting a diminutive Bonaparte in 1800 (above), while in 1820 a cartoon showed George IV in the unlikely situation of "the anticipation of a reconciliation" with his wife Caroline – all around him were his mistresses. Soon after their marriage in 1795 and the birth of Charlotte (who died in 1817) George and Caroline decided to live apart, with both continuing to have many lovers. When George IV became king in 1820 at 57, he denied Caroline entry to his lavish coronation. Queen Caroline still had huge popularity with the people, but was shunned in royal circles. However, in Scotland George was popular with the public (the two plates, right, with different colourings, were sold during his Scottish tour of 1822, when he donned a kilt).

A pearlware plate showed George taking his mistress to Carlton House, his London residence: riding the recently invented velocipede (or dandy-horse) c.1819.

Below: The Queen's Matrimonial Ladder, 1820, was an attack on George IV over a dispute with his wife, Queen Caroline, where the rungs of the ladder step from qualification to accusation, consternation and finally degradation.

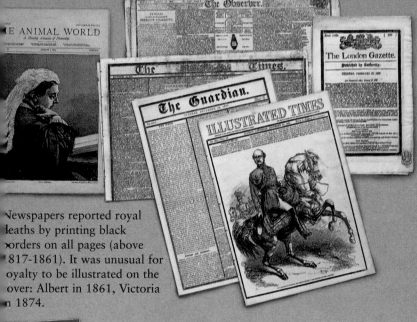

Newspapers reported royal deaths by printing black borders on all pages (above 1817-1861). It was unusual for royalty to be illustrated on the cover: Albert in 1861, Victoria in 1874.

Wider circulation of journals, magazines and books increased the interest in the royal family so that all through the twentieth century there was an avid market for special royal editions and commemorative issues (left). Publishers found that a royal face boosted sales, and new magazines were launched that just concentrated on royal matters, as did *The Throne* (1910) and *Royalty* (1981).

By the time of the silver jubilee of 1935, there was also an anti-monarchist press (above) being disparaging about money spent on the jubilee, or the need for a royal family. The press have often debated the role of the monarchy, sometimes putting over royal views (as in 1964), and sometimes interpreting for its readers, as *The Sun* did in 1992 with the Queen's 'annus horribilis'.

Royal patronage

For centuries, tradesmen and manufacturers aspired to link their businesses and products with royalty. The first known royal charter was granted in 1155 by Henry II to the Weavers' Company, and ever since royal warrants have been bestowed on favoured suppliers, especially during the reign of Queen Victoria. By the end of her reign some 1,080 firms used the royal coat of arms. During the late 1860s, advertisements began to appear actually flaunting royal personages giving that product added royal patronage. For example, Queen Victoria appeared to enjoy Cadbury's cocoa, Queen Alexandra tasted a Boisselier's chocolate and the entire royal family were, seemingly, fitted out in Anderson's waterproofs. The advertisement for A1 Sauce harked back to George IV's reign for royal approval.

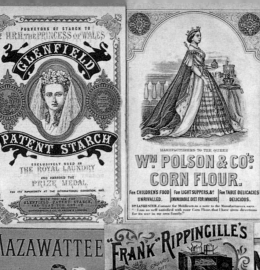

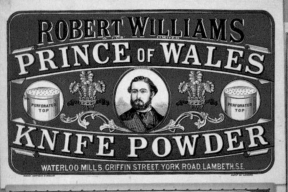

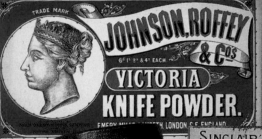

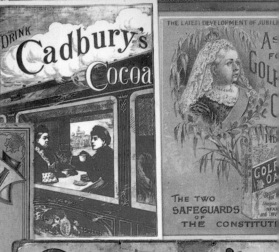

A royal image on the pack or used in the brand name gave kudos to any product. Some of the earliest images enlisted for everyday objects were those on needle boxes, such as the Duchess of Kent, Victoria's mother. Alexandra branded feeding bottles, tooth paste, pomade and oil.

Towards the end of Victoria's reign, the market for cigarettes was expanding rapidly, and royal connections were used to boost sales. A jubilee tin of Faulder's tobacco had been made for the Manchester exhibition of 1887. The Princess of Wales appeared on the lid of Elegant cigarettes, and Princess Mary of Teck, known as May, was used to promote May Blossom cigarettes from 1896. Wills launched Diamond Queen cigarettes in 1897 with an image of the monarch on the pack, and the following year the first set of kings and queens cigarette cards was issued by Wills (see advertisement). Many more sets were issued, along with special albums and commemorative boxes, the last series being in 1953 produced by Phillip Allman.

In 1894 the Prince of Wales accepted a casket of Terrabona tea at an exhibition at Olympia. The company made great use of this royal patronage, and the scene was incorporated into advertisements and their tea canisters, including one when Edward became king. To compete with these royal claims, Horniman's tea published images of Edward VII drinking their tea, 'a right royal drink'.

Royal chocolate boxes

Ever since the 1860s, fancy boxes of chocolates with pictorial lids have been on sale, especially during the Christmas season. In Victorian times, chocolates were comparatively expensive, but during the Edwardian era their popularity widened along with the introduction of milk chocolate. One of the earliest royal souvenir boxes of chocolates was that issued by A. J. Caley & Son of Norwich in 1896 to commemorate 'the longest reign in English history' (see page 11). For the Diamond Jubilee of 1897, Dunn's chocolate creams were sold in a small round tin (see page 14).

While there were a few commemorative chocolate boxes issued for Edward VII's coronation in 1902, especially by Fry's (see page 16), it was Cadbury's who launched the first regular box under a royal banner, King Edward chocolates. This assortment became King George chocolates (left) after the death of Edward, eventually becoming the most popular boxed chocolate of its time and imitated by other manufacturers. For the coronation of 1911 there were numerous souvenir boxes to mark the occasion, and this tradition was continued for the coronations of 1937 and 1953.

Connecting with royalty was good for business. In the 1920s Meltis created Duchess of York chocolates and then Little Princess chocolates (see page 29). Other manufacturers brought out further royal assortments such as Royal Highness, Duke of York, The Marys and Princess Elizabeth, but it was Prince of Wales chocolates that everyone wanted to produce during the 1920s and 1930s. Carson's called theirs Prince Edward, and Rowntree's used a famous photograph of the Prince of Wales smoking (the cigarette had been removed from the image on their box – see also page 28). To extend the royal connection even further, Rowntree's made Balmoral chocolates and, simply, Royal chocolates.

Queen Victoria

When Victoria became queen on 20 June 1837 at the age of 18, she succeeded her uncle, William IV. Her mother was the Duchess of Kent; her father had died in 1820, the third son of George III. Victoria would not have become queen had it not been for the death of Princess Charlotte (only daughter of the Prince Regent) in 1817, and the death of the 12-week-old daughter of the Duke of Clarence in 1821. Victoria married her cousin, Prince Albert of Saxe-Coburg-Gotha on 10 February 1840. Their first child was born on 21 November 1840, Princess Victoria (Vicky). Almost a year later, the queen gave birth to Albert. It was the first time that an English queen had given birth to a son and heir. The event was proclaimed in the streets (see right); in the journal *Fly* a print showed the royal couple 'at home' in Buckingham Palace.

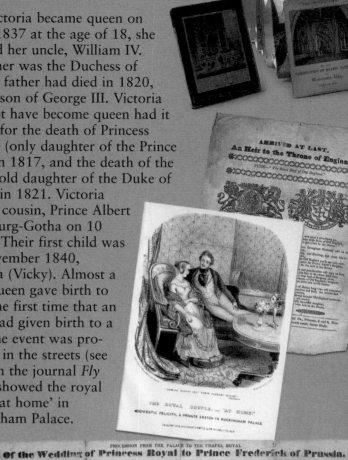

Souvenirs for Queen Victoria's coronation on 28 June 1838 included an 18-foot long panorama of the grand procession, a jigsaw, a peep show (top right) and salt-glaze stoneware gin flasks (on one the queen holds a scroll which reads 'may peace and prosperity prevail'). For the wedding of Victoria and Albert there were more souvenirs and another special issue of *The Sun* newspaper, but not printed in gold as the coronation issue had been.

A growing family: music cover, 1845; movable oak tree, 1846; Le Blond print,1848. Victoria's ninth child was born in 1857.

Souvenirs to mark the wedding of the Prince of Wales to Princess Alexandra, the attractive eldest daughter of Prince Christian of Denmark. The wedding was at Windsor on 10 March 1862.

Vicky, the Princess Royal, married Crown Prince Fredrick of Prussia on 25 January 1858 (the news of their engagement had been leaked two years earlier). They had a son a year later who became Kaiser Wilhelm of Germany. In 1862 Princess Alice married Louis IV Grand Duke of Hesse. All such events were marked by colourful song sheets (by the time that Maud of Wales married Prince Charles of Denmark in 1896, above, there were souvenir paper napkins, first seen in 1887). The queen's mother died in March 1861; Prince Albert died on 14 December 1861 of typhoid fever. He was 42.

By the end of Victoria's reign, progress had been immense, as illustrated on this cotton handkerchief, c.1896. The queen had enjoyed rail travel ever since her first journey in 1842.

In memory of Albert, the Prince Consort, the Royal Albert Hall was opened in 1871; the Albert Memorial in Kensington Gardens was completed in 1876. This marked the end of the queen's mourning for her late husband. As leader of the armed forces, her soldiers did their duty 'for queen and country'. A new medal 'for valour', the Victoria Cross, had been introduced in 1856 during the Crimean War. In 1900 she sent 100,000 tins of chocolate to her troops fighting in the Boer War (see above).

The Prince and Princess of Wales celebrated their silver wedding in 1888. A family dinner was held at Marlborough House; Alexandra was in good spirits with orange blossom in her hair and a real orange in its midst. She had dismissed from her mind her husband's liaisons with Lillie Langtry and others. Although there were no public celebrations (the court was in mourning for Vicky's husband, the German emperor), there were song sheets and a popular book on their lives was published.

Along with song sheets and Stevengraph bookmarks (made since the 1860s), the jubilees of 1887 and 1897 were celebrated by a growing souvenir business from product manufacturers like Barratt's sweets and Liebig – a mechanical card turned a cow into a jar.

Queen Victoria died on 22 January 1901 at Osborne House on the Isle of Wight (her favourite residence). She was 81 and had been queen for almost 64 years. Her funeral was recorded by numerous illustrations in magazines, by photographs and by the new medium of film.

In 1892 the Prince of Wales's est son, Albert, died of pneumonia. He had been engaged to Princess Mary of Teck. Prince George w courted Mary, and on 6 July 1893 they married at St. James's Palace. Mary's ents can be seen on the tin, above. Other tins, below, celebrated members of royal family.

During June 1887, the nation celebrated 50 years of Queen Victoria's reign, her Golden Jubilee. Everything went Jubilee mad; on the song sheet cover (far right), Gladstone appeared exasperated at the way every article had a jubilee tag, whether jubilee false teeth or jubilee frying pan. Fortunate children may have received a jubilee treat: a rubber ball or mug, or perhaps the school class was photographed.

Two firms, Raphael Tuck and Hildesheimer, published a series of relief scraps illustrating the principal events of the queen's reign. The mustard companies of Keen's and Colman's celebrated with advertisements and decorative tins; both firms had recently begun to issue such tin boxes for the Christmas trade, and the jubilee tins made a topical subject. Colman's tin has a continuous procession wrapped around the sides. Biscuit manufacturers also supplied seasonal gift tins; the examples here are from Huntley & Palmers, Macfarlane Lang and Carrs, with images of royal residences.

COLMAN'S MUSTARD

MANUFACTURERS TO H.M. THE QUEEN.
BY SPECIAL WARRANT

Sixty glorious years were celebrated at St. Paul's Cathedral on 22 June 1897, when Queen Victoria took part in the service to mark her Diamond Jubilee. This celebration was for the British people and the Empire, and accordingly the procession contained soldiers from every part of the Empire. There was the New Zealand Militia, Jamaican Artillery, Canadian Rifles, New South Wales Lancers, Natal Artillery, Cape Rifles and police from Hong Kong, the Straits Settlements and British Guiana. Now aged 78, Victoria had reigned longer than any other monarch, a record previously held by George III at 59 years.

Compared with the previous jubilee, there were many more souvenir mugs, including enamel ones, and ceramic plates were more often coloured, in contrast to the black and white prints before. The range of tins had also increased, with confectionery manufacturers like Parkinson, Callard & Bowser, Dunn and Guest andding their boxes to the mustard and biscuit firms. The tea company Mazawattee also produced two sizes of royal canister. For the first time, picture postcards had become part of the souvenir trade, while small trade cards were given to customers – the examples here were from Horniman's tea and Holloway's ointment. A novelty was the tin flag from Nestle's Swiss milk that could be spun to make a rattle. *The Daily Mail* newspaper (launched the previous year) published a special issue printed in gold.

Edward VII

On 9 August 1902, in a glittering coronation procession, Edward VII and Alexandra journeyed to Westminster Abbey from Buckingham Palace – the crowds were ecstatic, being held back by stout police-men, as recorded in the booklet (left) illustrated by the artist John Hassall. It had been 64 years since the last corona-tion. Due to his recent illness, the king was two stone lighter and the ceremony had to be shortened slightly. However, it was the frail 80-year old archbishop of Canterbury who felt the strain, nearly dropping the crown and almost putting it on the king's head the wrong way round.

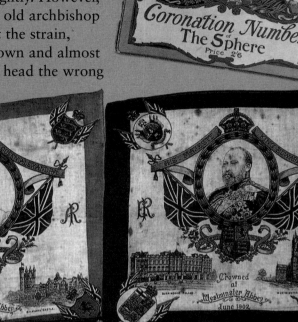

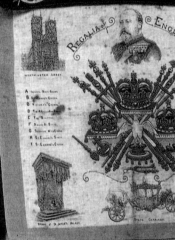

Edward VII became king on 23 January 1901, having rejected the title of Albert I which his mother would have preferred. The new king had a reputation for fast living, which included gambling and womanising, but the British public was devoted to the royal family and followed its lead in matters of dress and social tastes. There were two anxious moments early in Edward's reign. While sailing as a guest of Sir Thomas Lipton, the grocery millionaire, on board his racing yacht Shamrock II, a sudden squall snapped the mast during speed trials. Thankfully, no one was hurt. More serious, however, was when the king became seriously ill with appendicitis, having an operation on 24 June 1902. The coronation was due to have taken place two days later; it had to be postponed for six weeks (see poster below).

One of the many festivities in coronation year was when nearly 500,000 poor people were given a feast at 700 places all over London. Brewers contributed to the cost. Bass created their own King's Ale, a bottle of which can be seen on page 18. A proliferation of souvenirs included cotton handkerchiefs (above) and the Fry's chocolate box (left) with its movable coach and horses.

The royal family made frequent visits to towns and cities throughout the country, commemorated by chocolate tins, such as that for the opening of Royal Edward Dock in Bristol, 1908 (right). Empire Day was also celebrated with chocolate tins. In March 1901, George, Duke of York, was sent to Australia to open the first parlia-ment of this newly-created domin-ion. In November 1901 he became Prince of Wales and with his wife, Mary, made many royal visits at home and abroad such as that to India in 1906.

Along with the cracker label (left), royal images were popular on calendars given away by shop owners to their favoured customers. The image above, entitled 'Three Generations', shows the king and queen at the start of their reign with George and Mary and seven-year old son Edward. The king had determined not to impose the same strict discipline on his children from which he had suffered – George (now aged 36 on his father's accession), Louise (34), Victoria (32) and Maud (31). Their eldest son, Albert Victor, had died of typhoid in 1892. Edward was 59 when he became king, while Alexandra was 57. A keen sailor, Edward understood the importance of a strong navy and he endeavoured to initiate reforms within the Royal Navy. In 1906, the first of a new class of battleship, the Dreadnought, was launched. While this had followed the signing of the Entente Cordiale with France in 1904, when Edward was hailed as a peace maker, it was the growing tension with Germany's Kaiser Wilhelm, his nephew, that concerned him. In 1908 he became the first British king to visit Russia, where Tsar Nicholas II was Queen Alexandra's nephew and the Tsarina, the king's niece.

On 6 May 1910, Edward VII died suddenly from bronchitis at the age of 68.

At the time of Edward VII's coronation, the variety of souvenirs had continued to increase; the range of commemorative ceramic and tin mugs was now extensive. Mustard, biscuit, tea, tobacco and especially confectionery manufacturers sold their products in decorative tin boxes – firms represented here include Keen, Colman, Gray Dunn, Mazawattee, Horniman, Tower Tea (see above their embossed tin sign), Clarnico, Pascall, Rowntree (and on pages 20-21), Frys, Cadburys, Callard & Bowser, Tucker's butterscotch, and two tins from W. D. and H.O. Wills. Huntley & Palmers produced special coronation biscuits (on top of the large outer tin is a Colman's mustard pot made by Minton). A novel shoe box (below) shows the state opening of parliament in 1901 and "the king as he will appear in coronation robes".

Along with the electric illuminations, pocket puzzles and the new market for picture postcards, it was the colourful trade cards given away by shopkeepers that extended the festive mood. Examples here include those from Owbridges lung tonic, Lemco meat extract and Milkmaid Brand condensed milk (issued as school reward cards). Colman's produced a series of commemorative labels, each pasted onto the lids of their starch boxes: children could collect a series of twelve designs.

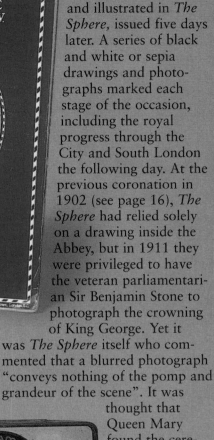

George V

As the nation mourned the death of Edward VII, George V succeeded his father in May 1910. Known as the sailor king, he often wore an admiral's uniform. As well as sailing and also shooting, another favourite pastime of his was collecting stamps, and he assembled what was perhaps the world's most comprehensive collection at the time. When crowned King of Great Britain and Ireland, the dominions beyond the seas and Emperor of India, George V became the first monarch to visit India since the honour had been bestowed on Queen Victoria (who never set foot there).

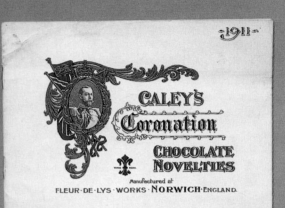

An example of the growing souvenir business: Caley's produced twelve different boxes of chocolates, and a special tin filled with chocolate biscuits (see page 25).

At the age of 17, the king's eldest son, Edward (but known as David by his family) was invested as Prince of Wales at Caenarvon Castle on 13 July 1911. It had been the first time for about 300 years that such an investiture was made, and the first at the castle. The seemingly ancient rituals were hurriedly devised.

On 22 June 1911, George V was crowned king at Westminster Abbey. The events of the day were described and illustrated in *The Sphere,* issued five days later. A series of black and white or sepia drawings and photographs marked each stage of the occasion, including the royal progress through the City and South London the following day. At the previous coronation in 1902 (see page 16), *The Sphere* had relied solely on a drawing inside the Abbey, but in 1911 they were privileged to have the veteran parliamentarian Sir Benjamin Stone to photograph the crowning of King George. Yet it was *The Sphere* itself who commented that a blurred photograph "conveys nothing of the pomp and grandeur of the scene". It was thought that Queen Mary found the ceremony an ordeal.

The king and queen made many visits around the country. A tour of industrial centres was organised during 1912, covering Yorkshire, South Wales and Bristol; some of these areas had seen unrest among the workers. More formal visits merited souvenir tins of chocolate, often given by the local mayor to schoolchildren; examples here come from Manchester, Preston, Accrington, Glasgow and Coatbridge. However, the outbreak of war in 1914 put a stop to these visits.

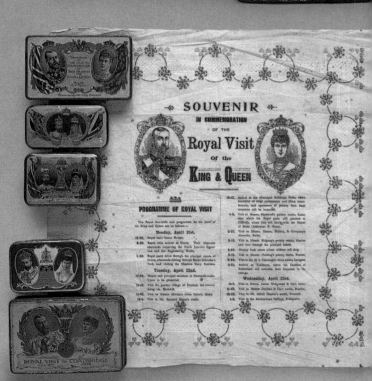

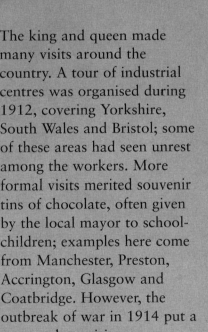

In 1915, there were celebrations for Prince Edward's 21st birthday. Souvenirs included tea canisters from Lyons and toffee caramels from Hartleys. The Prince of Wales was often depicted in naval uniform (as with his investiture); he had been at naval college for two years, from 1907 to 1909. However, in November 1914 he had become an aide-de-camp to General Sir John French, who was commanding the British Expeditionary Force. Eager to serve on the front line, he was given permission by his father to visit the trenches. He had wanted to serve with the Grenadier Guards but was prevented by Lord Kitchener.

First World War

When war was declared on Germany, the royal family took the lead in the nation's war effort. While Kitchener appeared on posters for recruitment, the king was seen as the nation's war leader. He frequently visited his troops at the front, and at home stopped dining out or going to the theatre, and prevented alcohol being served at royal residences. He even had his private garden converted to growing potatoes. Amongst many of her tasks, the Queen spent time organising comforts for the troops. One such was the sending of cigarettes, especially at

Christmas 1914, along with those from Queen Alexandra. It was Princess Mary's Christmas fund that provided cigarettes and tobacco in a brass tin (above).

While the Prince of Wales was in France (where on one occasion his driver was killed by shrapnel), Prince Albert saw action as a midshipman on board HMS Collingwood, which took part in the battle of Jutland. In the final weeks of the war, Albert joined the newly formed RAF as a staff officer at the front. When the war was won in November 1918, celebrating crowds gathered outside Buckingham Palace, where there was that "we have all been through this together" feeling.

"ALLIES IN ARMS"

Part 1.   6d. Net.

The GREAT WAR
THE STANDARD HISTORY OF THE ALL-EUROPE CONFLICT

Edited by H.W. Wilson, author of "With the Flag to Pretoria," "Japan's Fight for Freedom," etc.

L'UNION FAIT LA FORCE

HER ROYAL HIGHNESS
THE PRINCESS MARY'S
CHRISTMAS FUND
1914

CIGARETTES

HER ROYAL HIGHNESS
THE PRINCESS MARY'S
CHRISTMAS FUND
1914

TOBACCO

With Best Wishes for a Happy Christmas and a Happy New Year.

From The Princess Mary and Friends at Home

XMAS 1914

With best wishes from Alexandra

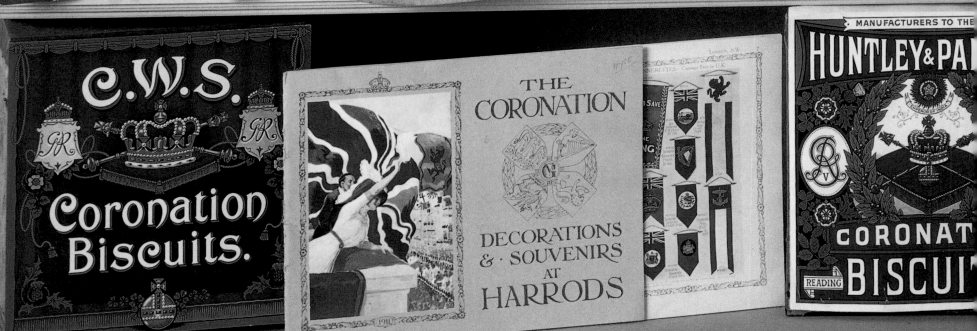

Now becoming a tradition, shops throughout the land were filled with decorations and souvenirs: flags, booklets, mugs, postcards, tin boxes and the unfolding procession pageantry. Portraits of George and Mary appeared everywhere, even on a card that promoted Black Cat cigarettes on the other side. The tins below were issued by the Co-operative Wholesale Society: biscuits (shaped), Mazawattee for tea, Caley's for biscuits and Callard & Bowser for nougat. A pair of figural mugs, made in Germany, made a small spelling error with 'H.M. Queen Mory'. But product promotion continually became intertwined with royal events. Thus *The Guide to the Coronation* was produced by Zam-Buk, "the world's standard healer and skin-cure". This booklet had useful tips on where best to see the royal procession ("the timber for stands would form a plank 4,500 miles long"), warnings on the dangers of London streets (171 fatal accidents caused by mechanical traffic in 1910), the romance of the anointing, and numerous stories of wondrous cures ("Zam-Buk: the only cure for crippling varicose vein ulcers").

Amongst the profusion of chocolate tins (note also the Fry's Coronation chocolate box wrapper), there were some tins for cigarettes, such as the two above, issued by Godfrey Phillips and W.D. and H.O. Wills. There was even a commemorative tin for hair pins (see centre). A new novelty was the embossed plaque (right) made from celluloid. Two artists showing their talent in this respect were Ernest Ibbotson, drawing scenes of the Lilliputian coronation and, in a book on King George V, Harry Payne, noted for his military illustrations. While fireworks were always part of royal festivities, a special tin filled with Brock's bangers made a popular appearance (shown here just below the catalogue for James Pain fireworks).

It will be seen from the fore-going that King George has been a great traveller, few men, if any, have seen more countries and met a more varied number of people representing the nations of the world. It has ever been his practice to study the manners and customs of those who inhabit his many dominions. It has also been his practice to associate himself with all the doings of his subjects. He is as earnest a soldier as he is an experienced sailor, and in this direction extends his interest to the boy scouts whom he inspected at Aldershot in 1910.

It has been written of His Majesty:

"Our present Sovereign is essentially an Imperial one. He knows the Empire, he understands it; no man living "knows or understands it better. "At home His Majesty has shown no "interest in the great commercial "industrial affairs of the country.

The Twenties

With Britain at peace, there was now a period of recovery. For the royal family, romance was in the air. The Prince of Wales had fallen in love with Freda Dudley Ward, but she was already married to a Liberal MP. Meanwhile Prince Albert (created Duke of York in 1920) became smitten by the charms of Lady Elizabeth Bowes-Lyon. But it was Princess Mary, the king's only daughter, who married first, to Viscount Lascelles, the eldest son of the Earl of Harewood. The wedding was held at Westminster Abbey on 28 February 1922. In 1924, the Queen's Dolls House was completed. Designed by Sir Edwin Lutyens, it was a marvel of miniaturisation. Housed at Windsor Castle, it could be seen for a 6d admission.

Souvenirs from the wedding included Sharp's and Mackintosh toffee. The mug dates from 1925 for the opening of a war memorial hospital at Whitby.

The prince's smiling face promoted many products, from chocolates and cigarettes to pins and fountain pens.

The Prince of Wales became the darling of the 'roaring twenties', setting fashion trends, golfing, flying and opening exhibitions, such as at Newcastle in 1929. He toured endlessly; on one trip he visited 46 countries.

The Duke of York married Elizabeth Bowes-Lyon on 27 April 1923. Previously, royal marriages had been held at Windsor, but now the procession to Westminster Abbey enabled a million people to watch.

The Daily Mirror 24 PAGES
NET SALE MUCH THE LARGEST OF ANY DAILY PICTURE NEWSPAPER
No. 6,077.   FRIDAY, APRIL 27, 1923.   One Penny.

LONG LIFE AND HAPPINESS!

THE ILLUSTRATED LONDON NEWS
PRICE TWO SHILLINGS.   The Illustrated London News: April 28, 1923.

LADY ELIZABETH BOWES-LYON   H.R.H. THE DUKE OF YORK

WEDDING NUMBER

Boys' Girls' Picture Newspaper
No. 1.—APRIL 23, 1923.   EDITED BY HAROLD WHEELER   TWOPENCE

OUR AIRMAN DUKE AND HIS BEAUTIFUL BRIDE

EDMONDSON'S RED SEAL COFFEE

Daily Mirror
$1,000 MUST-BE-WON RACING PRIZE: COUPON TO
THE DAILY PICTURE NEWSPAPER WITH THE LARGEST NET SALE
GREAT NEW SERIAL NEXT WEEK
No. 7,029   SATURDAY, MAY 22, 1926.   One Penny

FIRST PICTURE OF THE DUCHESS AND HER BABY

BABY'S PLATE
H.R.H. PRINCESS ELIZABETH
BORN APRIL 21ST 1926.

OUR EMPIRE'S LITTLE PRINCESS
BORN APRIL 21ST 1926.

Meltis DUCHESS OF YORK Assorted Chocolates
BEDFORD & LONDON, ENGLAND.

Meltis DUCHESS OF YORK Assorted Chocolates
HALF POUND (INCLUDING FOILS)

Meltis DUCHESS OF YORK Assorted Chocolates
LTD. BEDFORD & LONDON, ENGLAND.   HALF POUND (INCLUDING FOILS)

Meltis DUCHESS OF YORK ASSORTED CHOCOLATES

The Duchess of York soon became the society beauty of the decade, appearing on chocolate boxes produced by Meltis. The Duke and Duchess made many overseas tours – a safari holiday in Africa during 1924 and a tour of the West Indies, Pacific, New Zealand and Australia, where the Duke opened the new parliament building at Canberra. Their visit to Australia in 1927 was marked by a tin showing HMS Renown, produced by Hall's Duchess Assortment.

The Duke and Duchess's first child was a daughter they christened Elizabeth Alexandra Mary, born on 21 April 1926. It had been a difficult birth, delivered by caesarean section at the home of the duchess's parents in London. *The Daily Mirror* of 22 May devoted the whole front page to the "first picture of the Duchess and her baby". The young princess became the centre of public attention, appearing on a tasteful selection of pottery (the portrait of her aged two was by Marcus Adams), chocolate and cracker boxes. The little princess had accomplished the art of curtseying, and became known as 'Lilibet' because of the way she tried to pronounce her name.

The Duke of York suffered from a nervous stammer (although he took treatment from a speech therapist), and it made public speaking, such as the opening of the second year of the British Empire Exhibition in 1925, something of an ordeal. It was later in that year that Queen Alexandra died, aged 80.

Meltis LITTLE PRINCESS Assorted Chocolates
Meltis LTD. BEDFORD & LONDON, ENGLAND.
ONE POUND (INCLUDING FOILS)

LITTLE PRINCESS Assorted Chocolates
LTD. BEDFORD & LONDON, ENGLAND.
HALF POUND (INCLUDING FOILS)

TOM SMITH'S PRINCESS CRACKERS
MANUFACTURED IN ENGLAND BY TOM SMITH & CO LTD LONDON

Wife and Home

6 APRIL

Daily Mirror

THE DAILY PICTURE newspaper with the LARGEST NET SALE

No. 9,673 THURSDAY, NOVEMBER 29, 1934 One Penny

ROYAL WEDDING NUMBER

HERE'S HEALTH . . . . . . AND HAPPINESS!

The Nation's Toast To-day

Princess Elizabeth's Miniature House Built in Cardiff 1931

Queen Elizabeth's LITTLE HOUSE

PULL OUT STORY BOOK

WEEKLY ILLUSTRATED 2D

H.R.H. PRINCESS ELIZABETH.

PRINCESS ELIZABETH

H.R.H. PRINCESS MARGARET ROSE.

FROM A PORTRAIT BY MARCUS ADAMS

WEEKLY ILLUSTRATED 2D
Saturday, April 18, 1936. No. 42. VOL. II

DESCRIPTION OF THE BRIDE CAKE
made by
HUNTLEY & PALMERS, LTD.
for
H.R.H. PRINCESS MARINA OF GREECE
upon the occasion of her Marriage to
H.R.H. THE DUKE OF KENT
at
WESTMINSTER ABBEY
November 29th, 1934

Special View of Replica at
SELFRIDGES

The Thirties

On 21 August 1930, a second daughter, Margaret Rose, was born to the Duke and Duchess of York at Glamis Castle, Scotland. As the two princesses grew up, there was always public interest; they featured on magazine covers, jigsaws, mugs and cotton handkerchiefs. In 1931, the Welsh people built a little cottage (y bwthyn bach) for Princess Elizabeth; it toured for two years and was then given to the princess on her sixth birthday in 1933.

Another royal wedding was announced in 1934 when Princess Marina married George, Duke of Kent, at Westminster Abbey. Princess Elizabeth was a bridesmaid. The following year saw the celebrations for King George V's Silver Jubilee, focused on 6 May. A vast crowd gathered outside Buckingham Palace to sing *For He's a Jolly Good Fellow*. Throughout jubilee year, the king seemed genuinely surprised at the warm feeling from his subjects, and when he died on 20 January 1936, he was deeply mourned. In 1928 he had recovered from a serious illness, convalescing at Bognor (subsequently renamed Bognor Regis).

Daily Express

TODAY'S WEATHER: SHOWERY.

ROYAL FUNERAL MEMORIAL NUMBER

No.

WEDNESDAY, JANUARY 29, 1936

RADIO PROGRAMMES: PAGE 18.

ONE PENNY

SPECIAL PICTURE SUPPLEMENT
Pages 5, 6, 11, 12, 13

"SO ENDED THE REIGN OF KING GEORGE THE GOOD"

MR. LLOYD GEORGE DESCRIBES

Drama Of Last Scene At Windsor

"Stern, Simple Awe-Inspiring"

By The Right Hon.
DAVID LLOYD GEORGE, O.M.

The most famous man of his late Majesty's reign, his Prime Minister during its most troubled years, reports for the "Daily Express" the last farewell at St. George's Chapel, Windsor.

EARTH TO EARTH

FROM A SILVER BOWL KING EDWARD TOOK EARTH BROUGHT FROM THE CONSECRATED GROUND OF THE ROYAL BURIAL PLACE AT FROGMORE. SLOWLY HE SPRINKLED IT ON HIS FATHER'S COFFIN. GRADUALLY THE COFFIN SANK FROM SIGHT

PROGRAMME & GUIDE

of the
Funeral Procession
of our late beloved
King George V.
Born June 3rd 1865.
Passed away January 20th, 1936.

In Memoriam
HIS MAJESTY KING GEORGE V.

It is with deep regret,
He whom we all loved
as King has passed from
our midst. We offer our
profound sympathy to
Her Majesty The Queen
and the Royal Family

In Loving Memory of
H.M. KING GEORGE V
MONDAY, 20th JANUARY, 1936

In Loving Memory

WE SHALL NEVER FORGET

In Memoriam

PASSING OF A GREAT KING
Verses by Allan Junior

SILVER JUBILEE SOUVENIRS 25

THE ROYAL JUBILEE BOOK

The SILVER JUBILEE BOOK
25 YEARS ON THE THRONE

India

1910 SilverJubilee 1935

VANDYK. LONDON.

-PAGE JUBILEE No. of—
ANSWERS
Britain's National Weekly

In this Issue
8 PAGE ART PICTURE SOUVENIR of a Great Reign
2ᵈ

Long to Reign Over Us!

SILVER JUBILEE
PUNCH
PUNCH— May 1. 1935
No. 4899
VOLUME CLXXXVIII.
MAY 1
1935
1910 1935
SILVER JUBILEE

Jubilee The Envelope
1910 1935

For the Silver Jubilee, street parties flourished throughout Britain, and it seemed as if every magazine produced a special jubilee number. Woolworths printed a souvenir menu, encouraging customers that "this menu may be taken away". Chocolate bars were now adorned with royal wrappers, the CWS provided an embossed bar of soap (left), and jubilee envelopes were available (though the envelopes themselves were plain). For the first time, the Post Office issued royal commemorative stamps, along with stamp booklets and postal orders.

Abdication

Edward VIII became King at the age of 41, the only son of George V yet to marry, but the British public was unaware of the growing relationship with the married American, Wallis Simpson. The news broke to a stunned nation on 3 December 1936, and events unravelled in the newspaper headlines.

On 10 December, Edward signed the 'instrument of abdication', speaking the next day on the wireless about the woman he loved. Edward married Wallis Simpson in France on 3 June 1937… and as for the coronation mementoes – from a money box Oxo tin to designer mugs by Laura Knight and Eric Ravilious (top shelf, far right).

DEAD KING BEGINS HIS LAST JOURNEY—Page 3

DAILY SKETCH

No. 8,341 WEDNESDAY, JANUARY 22, 1936 ONE PENNY

PROCLAMATION DAY

KING EDWARD'S OATH TO NATION
'I am Determined to Follow in My Father's Footsteps'

His Council Told of The Queen's 'Overpowering Grief' at Loss

'FOR MY SUBJECTS'

Daily Mirror
THE DAILY PICTURE NEWSPAPER WITH THE LARGEST NET SALE

SATURDAY Dec. 15 · No. 10301 ONE PENNY

GOD SAVE THE KING!

TELL US THE FACTS, MR. BALDWIN!

"Suggestions have appeared that if the King decided to marry, his wife need not become Queen. These ideas are without any constitutional foundation."

Evening Standard
No. 35,030 LONDON, THURSDAY, DECEMBER 3, 1936 ONE PENNY

CHEDLET CHEESE AND CELERY

THE KING CALLS HIS STAFF TO FORT BELVEDERE

The Duchess of York Goes to See Queen Mary

MINISTERS MEETING TO-DAY

Daily Mirror
No. 10304 ONE PENNY

The four men who were in a vital conference with the King last night

THE KING AND BROTHERS HAVE FIVE - HOUR CONFERENCE WITH MR. BALDWIN AT FORT

M.P.s ARE GROWING MORE CHEERFUL

News Chronicle
No. 28,270 ONE PENNY FRIDAY, DECEMBER 4, 1936

TEST MATCH SPECIAL

BOURN-VITA for digestion, sleep and energy

THE KING: CRITICAL CONFERENCES
40-Minute Interview With Queen Mary Late Last Night

PREMIER SUMMONED TO PALACE AGAIN

| Message From Throne To Parliament? | Dukes of York, Kent and Gloucester Meet |

POSITION EASED AFTER ALL-DAY TALKS

EARLY THIS MORNING, AFTER A DAY AND NIGHT OF CONFERENCES, THERE WAS NO SOLUTION IN SIGHT OF THE PROBLEM RAISED BY THE KING'S DESIRE

Mrs. Simpson May Go Abroad

King May Broadcast
By the Radio Correspondent

LATEST TEST SCORE

"The Woman I Love"
THE ROMANCE OF EDWARD and WALLIS
Duke and Duchess of Windsor

The Star
THE LONDONER'S EVENING PAPER
No. 15,139. ONE PENNY. THURSDAY, DECEMBER 10, 1936. RADIO: Page Ten. WEATHER: Page Three.

EX-LAX For Constipation CHOCOLATE LAXATIVE

LATE FINAL

This is the Gin Gordon's Gin

SIR J. SIMON'S LAST MINUTE VISIT TO KING
Four Royal Brothers Together At Fort Belvedere

THE ACCESSION COUNCIL READY TO MEET

Crowded House To Hear Mr. Baldwin Read Royal Statement

DOMINIONS TOLD OF DECISION

The King May Broadcast To The Nation To-morrow

MR. BALDWIN.

ABDICATION ANNOUNCED

GREAT WHITEHALL CROWD
Street Cleared

The Evening News
LARGEST EVENING NET SALE IN THE WORLD
NO. 17,134 LONDON : THURSDAY, DECEMBER 10, 1936 ONE PENNY

LATE NEWS! Yeast-Vite LATE EXTRA

THE KING ABDICATES
"My Final And Irrevocable Decision" Communicated In A Message To Parliament

"I CAN NO LONGER DISCHARGE MY HEAVY TASK WITH EFFICIENCY"

Abdication Instrument Signed To-day With The Three Royal Brothers as Witnesses

SENSATIONAL SPEECH BY MR. BALDWIN

"The King Told Me, 'I Am Going To Marry Mrs. Simpson And I Am Prepared To Go'"

PROCLAIMING NEW KING
ON SATURDAY MORNING

KING EDWARD GO ABROAD

Daily Mirror
No. 10306 ONE PENNY

LATE · LON · ED

EDWARD VIII'S RADIO FAREWELL TO-NIGHT

THIS ISSUE IS HISTORIC - PRESERVE IT!

NEWS Review
Britain's First Weekly Newsmagazine

Wallis

London Cheers George VI

Edward VIII will broadcast to the Empire and the world to-night as Mr. Edward Windsor, a "private individual owing allegiance to the new King."

This will follow the signing of his abdication papers and the succession to the Throne of his brother, the Duke of York, who will be 41 on Monday.

The time has been fixed tentatively for 10 p.m. During the evening Edward VIII is expected to leave the country.

DAILY SKETCH
No. 8,765 FRIDAY, JUNE 4, 1937 ONE PENNY

Simply say SEAGERS GIN

THE DUKE'S Wedding Pictures

The KING and the LADY

THREE KINGS IN ONE YEAR

Why did Edward VIII abdicate? — Facts which were not told

6ᴰ

Prince Edward's Farewell to the Nation

Daily Mirror
No. 10452 ONE PENNY

FRIDAY, JUNE 4, 1937

LATE · LON · ED

... The Duke and Duchess of Windsor ...

ON THE STEPS OF A NEW LIFE—TOGETHER

Souvenir Book
KING EDWARD VIII
TOLD IN PICTURES

Including his Abdication Message and Broadcast Speech

EDWARD VIII

KING   EMPEROR

SOUVENIR
OF HIS
ABDICATION
Dec. 10ᵗʰ 1936

KING EDWARD VIII
CORONATION SOUVENIR
1937

HIS MOST EXCELLENT MAJESTY
EDWARD THE EIGHTH

WEEKLY
ILLUSTRATED
2ᴰ

The Evening News

Dunville's
OLD IRISH WHISKY

LARGEST EVENING NET SALE IN THE WORLD

KING EDWARD VIII FLIES TO LONDON
The First British Monarch Ever to Travel by Air

PROCLAIMING THE NEW
KING

SPECIAL MEETING OF THE PRIVY COUNCIL AT
ST. JAMES'S PALACE THIS AFTERNOON

KING GEORGE LYING IN STATE

HIS BODY WILL BE BROUGHT BACK TO LONDON
ON THURSDAY

H.M.
KING EDWARD
SPECIALLY ENLARGED
SOUVENIR NUM

KING EDWARD
CHOCOLATES

Cadbury's
KING EDWARD
CHOCOLATES

CORONATION 1937   CORONATION 1937

FRY'S
MILK
CHOCOLATE
6ᴰ

FRY'S MILK CHOCOLATE 6ᴰ

Coronation
May 12ᵗʰ 1937

For the coronation that never happened, a vast array of souvenirs were already on sale at the time of Edward VIII's abdication: pin badges and medallions, cotton handkerchiefs and paper serviettes, pen knives, a hair brush and pocket mirror, cuff links, and even a small sewing kit containing thimble, cotton and needles.

George VI

On the abdication of his brother, the Duke of York became king on 12 December 1936. At the age of 41, he had not expected, or wanted, to be king, but the throne was now thrust upon him. He took his father's name George to emphasise continuity. George VI was determined to do his duty even though he was a shy man, still with a slight stammer, and Queen Elizabeth and Queen Mary were both there beside him.

Coronation day was set as the one originally intended for Edward VIII: 12 May 1937. Huge numbers of people turned out to line the processional route; for those who could not see, periscopes were available (see examples on pp. 42-43). However, for the first time, a radio broadcast of the day's events was made, and the embryonic television service relayed black and white pictures of the returning procession from Hyde Park Corner. There were just 2,100 TV sets in use at the time. Photographs were rushed into publications, and the king made a radio broadcast to the Empire in the evening.

Selfridges decorated their store to glorious effect, and every description of souvenir went on sale: a record of stirring music (below), pocket powder compact, paper Sifta Salt hat, Neptune orange drink and Strawson's Coronation Poles. *Woman's World* published a cakes and pastries guide with free pack of mixed spice, and the whole occasion was typified by the song *We shall all be there on Coronation Day.*

The king and queen made a royal tour of Canada and the U[SA] during May and June 1939. It was a great success and helped build bridges between the UK and USA. Over 50,000 people cheered their return outside Buckingham Palace.

WEEKLY ILLUSTRATED 2d

THE QUEEN AND HER DAUGHTERS

ILLUSTRATED 2d

ROYAL CHILDREN
Snapshot Album

QUEEN MARY 70TH BIRTHDAY NUMBER

Prizes for "Snapshot" Stories
HOME CHAT 2d

A Picture to Keep

With turbulent times at home and abroad, this close-knit family (referred to by the king as 'us four') put on an air of business as usual. Dolls of the princesses were made by Chad Valley. In 1939, Princess Elizabeth was 13 years old, 'learning to be queen', while Margaret was 9: "full of fun and high spirits, with a natural courtesy and charm".

WOMAN'S OWN 2d EVERY FRIDAY

Princess Margaret Rose

Learning to be a Queen
WOMAN'S OWN 2d EVERY FRIDAY April 29, 1939

Amongst the mementoes for the occasion were a pack of red, white and blue sweet peas, a giant ten-inch pencil, a Boston garter with the king's image on the lid, and a walnut containing sixteen miniature photographs of the royal family. There was also a mechanical procession on clear celluloid strips, where the coach and horses moved in one direction and aeroplanes flew overhead in the other. Along with better black and white photographs in *The Spectator*, there were now colour illustrations, and the whole ceremony was also recorded on film from behind sound-proof glass.

Many of the souvenirs prepared for Edward VIII were modified for George VI's coronation; compare the designs of tins and mugs with those on page 35. Along with the seaside buckets, money boxes, paper plates and postcards, food manufacturers joined the celebrations. Hartley's table jellies made a Buckingham Palace box with a rotating wheel that put one of four royal faces on the balcony; Smith's Crisps designed a special bag and also, for two pence, Lyons' Coronation Kup vanilla ice cream was available. A royal toast could also be made with Simonds' coronation brew – in an innovative beer can – or with non-alcoholic champagne Cheerio ('a kingly drink'), or just with milk, where Express Dairy were at pains to point out that "there will only be one delivery made on Wednesday, May the 12th" (normally two deliveries were made daily).

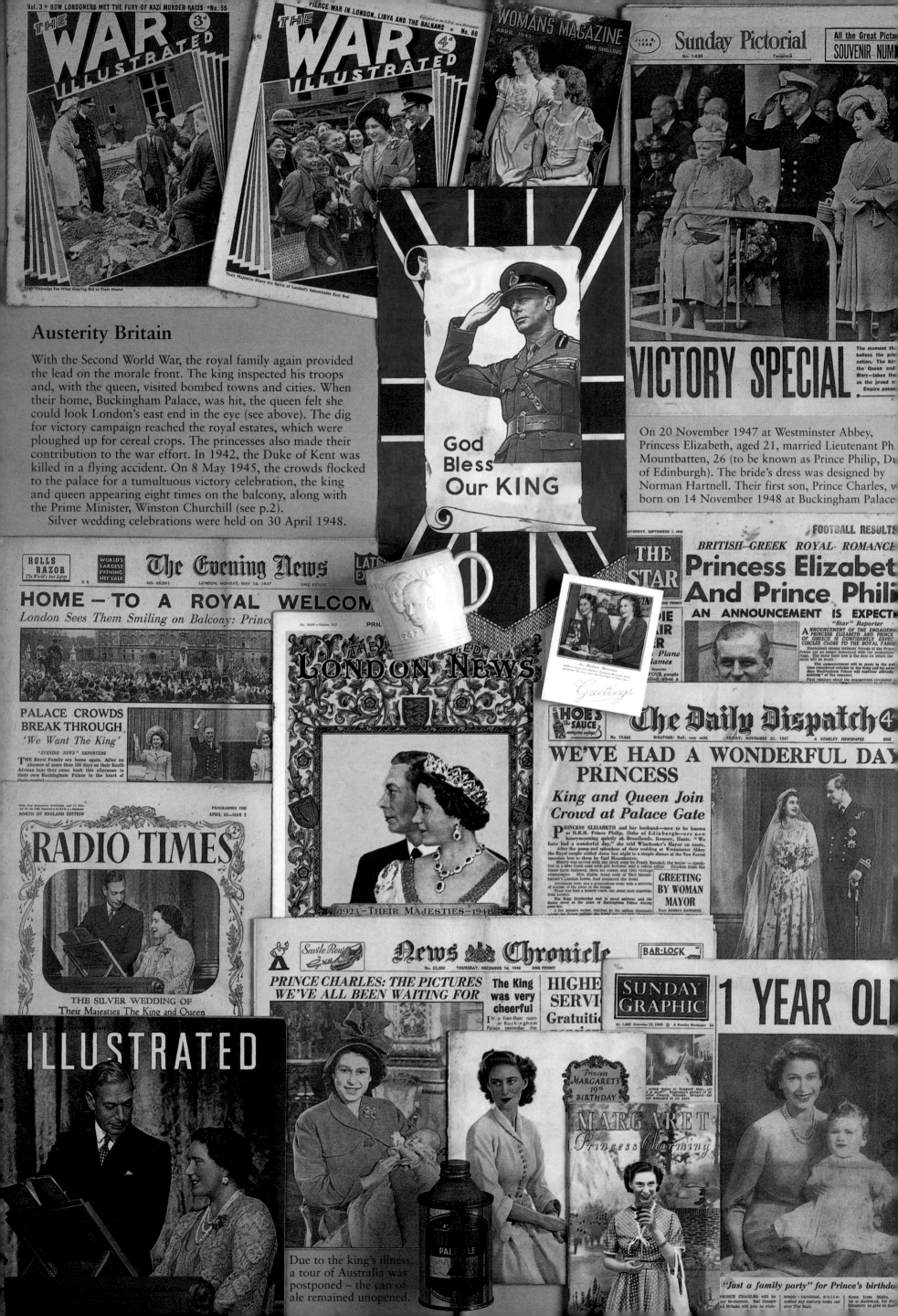

THE WAR ILLUSTRATED
3d Weekly

Their Majesties See What Goering Did to Their Home

THE WAR ILLUSTRATED
4d Weekly
FIERCE WAR IN LONDON, LIBYA AND THE BALKANS   No. 88

Their Majesties Share the Spirit of London's Indomitable East End

WOMAN'S MAGAZINE
ONE SHILLING
APRIL 1943

Sunday Pictorial
JUNE 9, 1946   No. 1,630   Twopence
All the Great Pictures
SOUVENIR NUMBER

VICTORY SPECIAL

The moment the bullocs the pri... nation. The Ki... the Queen and Mary—takes the as the proud m... Empire passe...

Austerity Britain

With the Second World War, the royal family again provided the lead on the morale front. The king inspected his troops and, with the queen, visited bombed towns and cities. When their home, Buckingham Palace, was hit, the queen felt she could look London's east end in the eye (see above). The dig for victory campaign reached the royal estates, which were ploughed up for cereal crops. The princesses also made their contribution to the war effort. In 1942, the Duke of Kent was killed in a flying accident. On 8 May 1945, the crowds flocked to the palace for a tumultuous victory celebration, the king and queen appearing eight times on the balcony, along with the Prime Minister, Winston Churchill (see p.2).

Silver wedding celebrations were held on 30 April 1948.

God Bless Our KING

On 20 November 1947 at Westminster Abbey, Princess Elizabeth, aged 21, married Lieutenant Ph... Mountbatten, 26 (to be known as Prince Philip, Du... of Edinburgh). The bride's dress was designed by Norman Hartnell. Their first son, Prince Charles, w... born on 14 November 1948 at Buckingham Palace...

The Evening News
ROLLS RAZOR — The World's Best Safety
WORLD'S LARGEST EVENING NET SALE
NO. 20,361   LONDON, MONDAY, MAY 12, 1947   ONE PENNY

HOME — TO A ROYAL WELCOME
London Sees Them Smiling on Balcony: Prince

PALACE CROWDS BREAK THROUGH
'We Want The King'

'EVENING NEWS' REPORTERS

THE Royal Family are home again. After an absence of more than 100 days on their South African tour they came back this afternoon to their own Buckingham Palace in the heart of their capital...

THE ILLUSTRATED LONDON NEWS
No. 6149—Volume 213

1923 — THEIR MAJESTIES — 1948

THE STAR
FOOTBALL RESULTS
BRITISH—GREEK ROYAL ROMANCE
Princess Elizabet... And Prince Phili...
AN ANNOUNCEMENT IS EXPECT...

"Star" Reporter

AN ANNOUNCEMENT of the engagement of PRINCESS ELIZABETH AND PRINCE OF GREECE IS CONFIDENTLY EXPEC... CIRCLES CLOSE TO THE ROYAL FAMI...

The Daily Dispatch
HOE'S SAUCE everybody enjoys!
No. 14,465   WEATHER: Dull, very mild.   FRIDAY, NOVEMBER 21, 1947   A Kemsley Newspaper   One

WE'VE HAD A WONDERFUL DAY
PRINCESS

King and Queen Join Crowd at Palace Gate

PRINCESS ELIZABETH and her husband—now to be known as H.R.H. Prince Philip, Duke of Edinburgh—are now honeymooning quietly at Broadlands, Romsey, Hants. "We have had a wonderful day," she told Winchester's Mayor en route...

GREETING BY WOMAN MAYOR
From AUBREY HAMMOND

RADIO TIMES
2d
PROGRAMMES FOR APRIL 25—MAY 1
NORTH OF ENGLAND EDITION

THE SILVER WEDDING OF Their Majesties The King and Queen

News Chronicle
Savile Row
No. 32,500   THURSDAY, DECEMBER 16, 1948   ONE PENNY
BAR-LOCK

PRINCE CHARLES: THE PICTURES WE'VE ALL BEEN WAITING FOR

The King was very cheerful
IN a first-floor room at Buckingham Palace yesterday the...

HIGHE... SERVI... Gratuitie...

SUNDAY GRAPHIC
No. 1,502 November 13, 1949   A Kemsley Newspaper   2d

1 YEAR OL...

ILLUSTRATED

Due to the king's illness, a tour of Australia was postponed – the can of ale remained unopened.

Princess MARGARET'S 19th BIRTHDAY
MARGARET Princess Charming

"Just a family party" for Prince's birthda...

PRINCE CHARLES will be..

THE STAR
Latest Prices

LATE FINAL

THE PRINCESS SAYS "I WILL"

SOUVENIR COVER

E. West,
Poste Restante,
Charing Cross,
W.C.2.

ROYAL WEDDING
20th November, 1947

PRINCESS ELIZABETH'S WEDDING DAY

THE ROYAL COUPLE LEAVING WESTMINSTER ABBEY

THE ILLUSTRATED LONDON NEWS
ROYAL WEDDING NUMBER

No. 1662—Volume 211

By Gracious Permission of His Majesty the King

THE WEDDING OF
HER ROYAL HIGHNESS
PRINCESS ELIZABETH
AND LIEUTENANT
PHILIP MOUNTBATTEN, R.N.

MINSTER ABBEY, 20th NOVEMBER 1947

SOUVENIR 2/6 PROGRAMME

RADIO TIMES
JOURNAL OF THE BBC
PRICE TWOPENCE

PROGRAMMES FOR
NOVEMBER 16—22

THE ROYAL WEDDING

ILLUSTRATED

A Souvenir JIGSAW
by Lumar

MADE IN GREAT BRITAIN

Royal Romance
THE STORY OF ELIZABETH & PHILIP
BY VINCENT

THE ROYAL WEDDING IN PICTURES
Abbey Ceremony by H. V. Morton

The Fifties

Though rationing was still evident, the worst was over and the nation's morale was boosted by the Festival of Britain, opened by the king in May 1951. On 15 August 1950, Princess Elizabeth had given birth to her second child, Anne. The family gathering recorded the recent arrival in the jigsaw puzzle below. For trooping the colour in June 1951, Elizabeth represented her father, who was ill; in July Prince Philip left the Royal Navy and in October both toured Canada. It was while Elizabeth and Philip were on tour in Africa that George VI died. They were staying at Treetops in the Kenyan bush when the news broke.

The Evening News

THE KING DIES IN HIS SLEEP AT SANDRINGHAM

Passed Away Peacefully This Morning

At the age of 56, the king died on 6 February 1952, after a long illness. He had recently been operated on for lung cancer, had been a heavy smoker for many years.

DAILY HERALD

THREE VEILED QUEENS WAIT

The King in state where his people pay homage today

On 16 February 1952, the nation observed two minutes' silence for the king's funeral. The Queen became Queen Elizabeth the Queen Mother.

Elizabeth II

Heralded as the dawn of a new Elizabethan era, the coronation was held on 2 June 1953 – the spirits of the nation were lifted even though the weather was overcast and wet. With two million lining the processional route, there were also 20 million at home huddled around the television sets of those fortunate enough to have one. For the first time, the masses could see the actual crowning ceremony and the ritual anointment with holy oil (made to a formula dating back to Charles I). Queen Mary had hoped to attend the ceremony, but died three months before, aged 85.

In the years that followed, the Queen with Prince Philip toured the Commonwealth – Australia and New Zealand in 1954, African colonies in 1956, Canada in 1959. In 1957 they visited the USA. But for Princess Margaret, there was heartache after the end of her romance with Group Captain Peter Townsend. In 1957, the Duke of Edinburgh's Award Scheme began, and at Christmas that year the Queen's broadcast was seen on television for the first time.

Daily Mirror
DEATH OF QUEEN MARY

With an extra 100,000 television sets bought in time for the coronation, there were around two million homes equipped to view the procession and the ceremony inside Westminster Abbey, all commentated on by Richard Dimbleby.

DAILY EXPRESS
QUEEN'S DAY—TV'S DAY
'This gleaming lady' and her Prince wave from balcony

A varied range of souvenirs included paper dolls, kitchen apron, brush and mirror set and embroidered towel, but the new material was hygienic plastic. Items included table cloths, crown-shaped painting sets and plastic coronation coach, palace and abbey mounted on the processional route.

QUEEN ELIZABETH SCRAP BOOK

Coronation SCRAP BOOK 1953

Filling scrapbooks has been a favourite pastime since Victorian times, particularly amongst children. The opened book above was compiled by Robert Opie, aged 5, containing pictures from magazines and newspapers, advertisements like Spangles and Double Diamond, milk bottle tops and bread wrapper decorations (he won first prize at school for his efforts).

Headscarves were a trendy fashion accessory during the 1950s. These three silk scarves (right) made the most of a two and a half foot square of material. The book (left) with 'realistic pop-up pictures' told a story of how John and Ann had come to London to see the coronation. The story told how it was the Duke of Buckingham whose house, built in 1702, was bought by George III in 1762, but not used regularly until Edward VII's reign.

Periscopes were a useful aid to those who could not see above the crowd in front. Some promoted products such as Weston's biscuits, Cope's tobacco and Hovis bread. In 1937 there was a periscope issued by United Dairies (see p. 42).

issued by United Dairies (see p. 42).

Retailers vied with each other to create a festive feel in their shop windows, filling them with flags, streamers and patriotic bunting. The products too caught the mood of the moment. Sliced bread was now widely available, and many bakeries used commemorative wrappers. With a bit of perseverance, it was possible to find, and cut out, the whole procession from the backs of the Welgar Shredded Wheat boxes. Crosbies' marmalade came in coronation mugs, and there was a special Easter egg box. United Dairies urged their customers to put out their empties.

Shopping in 1953 was made the more fun by discovering how many different coronation paper bag designs there were. Some harked back to Elizabeth I, others focused on the royal coach or the Queen's head.

TIMES

PRICE THREEPENCE

Radio Times (Broadcasting World Radio)   May 29, 1953
Vol. 119. No. 1543. Registered at the G.P.O. as a Newspaper

RADIO TIMES

BBC SOUND AND TELEVISION
PROGRAMMES..MAY 31—JUNE 6   3ᵈ

TV mirror

E II R
1953

CORONATION NUM—

The Queen on Television
★

... holiday and special Coronation broadcasts
... 'Henry V,' 'The Importance of Being Earnest,'
... ert from Royal Festival Hall, 'The Queen's People,'
... Television's All-Star 'Coronation Music-Hall'

ALONG LONDON'S PROCESSIONAL WAY: pages 6-7

CORONATION SOUVENIR
NEEDLE BOOK
25 NEEDLES
MADE IN ENGLAND

FRY'S CHOCOLATE CREAM

London Scenes
CORONATION · 1953
In Fine Toilet Soap

Coronation
PLAIN YORK CHOCOLATE
THE DUKE'S BAT
ROWNTREE'S
CORONATION PLAIN YORK CHOCOLATE 2d

TION OF HER MAJESTY QUEEN ELIZA
JUNE   CORONATION   1953

CROWN the QUEEN
CARD GAME
THE QUEEN
TRUMPETER
INVENTED BY
ELAINE BURTON
MEMBER OF PARLIAMENT
RULES ENCLOSED
POL

Royal Pageant

BY AIR MAIL
PAR AVION
AIR LETTER
AEROGRAMME
ER
1953
CORONATION

Weetabix

A GRAND STAND!
FOR COOKING AND SEASONING
OXO CUBE
OXO - AT ALL TIMES

LONG LIVE THE QUEEN

MAY 2 1953   EVERY WEDNESDAY FOURPENCE
ILLUSTRATED

12/11 INC. P.T.
Coronation 1953
12/11

THE QUEEN: Man Who
Took The New Pictures
SEE INSIDE

CORONATION
Painting Book

OUR QUEEN
Transfer Story Book

Adding to the excitement and
anticipation, coronation souvenirs
appeared everywhere. The sweet
ration had just ended, and many
chocolate bars had commemorative
wrappers. Dorothy Wilding's portrait
of the Queen (top left corner) became
the classic image. *The Radio Times*
showed the crowning decorations
erected along The Mall, and their
coronation number was illustrated by
Eric Fraser, who also designed the
Huntley & Palmers biscuit tin (see
p.50–51, top centre). The Royal
Pageant stationery box rotates a
procession through the TV screen.

CORONATION KNITTING SET
COLOURED BALLS OF WOOL · KNITTING PINS · CORONATION CUT-OUT

CORONATION

Models of the royal state coach were a popular souvenir, and the image was used on many story book covers, and even translated into a commemorative teapot. A circular jigsaw puzzle was a novel idea, as was a money box in the shape of a crown ("approved by the council of Industrial Design"). The loving-cup – "Here's health unto Her Majesty" – was made by Royal Doulton for Courage brewers and designed by Milner Gray. Just to prove how any utility object could become a coronation souvenir, look at the Fusilier lighter (a flint device to light the gas cooker).

SPECIAL WEDDING SOUVENIR
PRESENTATION 14" x 18" COLOUR PHOTOGRAPH INSIDE

DAILY EXPRESS
FRIDAY MAY 6 1960   Price 2½d.

Midnight: London is stopped
—and even the M.P.s stop talking

WHAT A NIGHT

Clarence House 'siege'

Express Staff Reporter

LONDON had a party last night—a roaring, jam-packed, do-as-you-like party for today's royal wedding.

And as a result: PRINCESS MARGARET—H.R.H. the Bride—was besieged in Clarence House.

THE HOUSE OF COMMONS had to suspend its sitting.

THE WEST-END was jammed solid with cars and crowds and with people camping out on the route for today's

I predict

Evening Standard
FRIDAY MAY 6 1960

All England here, whose symbol is the Rose
Prays that this Lady's Fortune may be fai...

JOHN MASEFIELD

Two hands wave in unison. Two smiles that mean only happiness. The radiant Princess and her husband go on to the balcony at Bucking... Palace to acknowledge the cheers of the massive crowd as one of the little bridesmaids looks up in astonishment.

WE DID NOT KNOW SHE COULD BE SO LOVELY

By ANNE SHARPLEY

Honeymoon yacht moves to a Thames salute

RADIO TIMES
TELEVISION BBC AND SOUND   MAY 1—7

PRICE FOURPENCE

THE ROYAL WEDDING
The Service in Westminster Abbey and the scenes along the processional route

Princess Margaret's WEDDING BOOK

ROYAL ROMANCE

Watched by a worldwide television audience of 200 million, Princess Alexandra (26), the Queen's cousin, married Angus Ogilvy on 24 April 1963 (below).

PRINCESS MARGARET'S WEDDING DAY

TODAY
6d

SECRET FATE OF PETER...
THE AVENGER DRESSES A...
—gay new feature for men...
ERSKINE CALDWELL'S FRA...
NO...

THE WEDDING IN COLOUR: Eight pages to t...

THE ROYAL BRIDE AND THE BRIDEGROOM

The Sixties

A fairy-tale wedding for Princ... Margaret, aged 29. Wearing a dress by Norman Hartnell, sh... married society photographer Antony Armstrong-Jones on 6 May 1960 at Westminster Abbey. They honeymooned on the royal yacht Britannia, whi... sailed to the Caribbean. Their son, Viscount Linley, was born in 1961 and a daughter, Lady Sarah, in 1964.

The first royal wedding to tak... place in York for 600 years ha... pened on 8 June 1961 (below... when a cousin of the Queen, t... Duke of Kent (25), married Katharine Worsley (28).

THE ROYAL WEDDING
First great COLOUR pictures!

THE ILLUSTRATED LONDON NEWS

PRICE TWO SHILLINGS AND SIXPENCE

God Bless the Prince of Wales.

Investiture of the Prince of Wales

Although he became Prince of Wales in 1958, Prince Charles was not actually invested as such until he was 20 years old, when he became the 21st Prince of Wales. The ceremony took place at Caernarvon Castle on 1 July 1969, and was televised to a 200 million worldwide audience.

1969 PRINCE'S ALE

H.R.H. THE DUKE OF KENT AND MISS WORSLEY

The Seventies

During her tour of New Zealand and Australia in 1970, Queen Elizabeth began to make a point of walking over to the crowds and talking to them; the era of the walk-about had begun. Meanwhile, Princess Anne had become an accomplished horse rider, winning the three-day event at Burghley on her horse Doublet. She was voted BBC sports personality of the year in 1971.

Sports Personality of the Year Jigsaw

H.R.H. The Princess Anne on 'Doublet' JIGSAW SIZE APPROX. 11"×9"
100 PIECES

Evening Standard
London : Tuesday May 29 1973   CLOSING PRICES

ANNE WILL WED MARK

—announcement tonight?

Evening Standard Souvenir   10p

MARK AND ANNE

The Royal Wedding watched by the world

— 24 pages of pictures and articles

Mark: I was petrified when I asked Prince Philip

ANNE — OUR LOVE STORY

By DOUGLAS DUMBRELL
Press Association Court Correspondent

PRINCESS ANNE and her fiance Lieutenant Mark Phillips strolled across the lawns at Buckingham Palace today and talked to me about their engagement. First of all, the Princess showed me the sapphire...

ROYAL WEDDING 1973
ANNE   MARK

H.R.H. PRINCESS ANNE   CAPT. MARK PHILLIPS

The wedding of Her Royal Highness
The Princess Anne
and
Captain Mark Phillips
Westminster Abbey November 14, 1973

King George's Jubilee Trust
Published by Gracious permission of Her Majesty the Queen

NOVEMBER 14th 1973

Watched by an estimated world-wide television audience of 500 million, Princess Anne, aged 23, became the first of the Queen's children to marry. She had fallen for Captain Mark Phillips (25); the wedding took place at Westminster Abbey on 14 November 1973. Both husband and wife were keen equestrians; Mark Phillips was part of the winnng team at the three–day event in the Munich Olympics of 1972, and Princess Anne also took part, becoming the first member of the royal family to compete at an Olympics. In 1977 she gave birth to her first child, Peter, and in 1981 Zara was born. It was during the Seventies that the Duke of Windsor (the former King Edward VIII) died in Paris in 1972 at the age of 77; in 1979 Earl Mountbatten of Burma was killed by an IRA bomb while on a fishing boat off the Irish coast.

A flood of souvenirs for the 1977 jubilee: beads, belt, paintbox, maths set, postage stamps and a peep show: a throwback to Victorian times (see p.10).

While the slogan "Liz rules - OK?" was painted on walls and printed in *Woman's Own*, and *Fab 208* waved the flag announcing "The Queen Rules, OK!", there was anti-jubilee sentiment, and some republicans wore 'stuff the jubilee' badges. *The New Statesman* ran an anti-monarchy issue. On Jubilee day, the punk group The Sex Pistols released a single called 'God Save The Queen', a monarchy-bashing anthem which, despite being boycotted, reached No. 2 in the charts.

Fab 208
The Queen Rules, O.K.!
In double page colour
Plus Part 3 of our Beauty Course
"It's the little things I miss most" Says a Fab reader whose father was made redundant

GOD SAVE THE QUEEN
Sex Pistols

SHE AINT NO HUMAN BEIN'

SEX PISTOLS

HER MAJESTY'S Silver Jubilee
To Celebrate
1952   CORONATION   1977

SOUVENIR
The Queens Silver Jubilee

Silver Jubilee Soft Margarine
JUBILEE BEADS
Cadbury's MILK TRAY

THE QUEEN'S SILVER JUBILEE
1952   1977

ER   SILVER   JUBILEE   ER

54

Despite the economic troubles, inflation and unemployment, the Silver Jubilee of 1977 found Britain in festive mood. Jubilee year saw the Queen visit many Commonwealth countries, and she travelled some 7,000 miles around Britain, including Northern Ireland. Jubilee day was held on 7 June; the night before, the Queen had lit a bonfire at Windsor to start a chain of fires from Land's End to the Shetlands. Thousands of street parties were held, set up on trestle tables laden with cakes and red, white and blue jelly – see the cover of *Buster* comic below.

Manufacturers and supermarkets caught the spirit of the time, creating special packs and products, such as the Co-op's Jubilade drink and Jubilee soft margarine, Lyons Maid red, white and blue iced lollies, Findus Silver Jubilee mousse and Bird's Eye's patriotic trifle. Many brands offered appropriate souvenir gifts like Branston with a pickle spoon, Crown paint with a Jubilee crown coin and Ovaltine with a colouring book or commemorative mug. Some London buses were painted silver, and toy models went on sale. Children could wear special socks, and for the baby there was even a souvenir bib. Surprisingly, there was little from the confectionery industry, no chocolate wrappers and few small decorative tins.

The Eighties

With the announcement of the engagement on 24 February 1981, Prince Charles ended months of speculation that he was going to marry Lady Diana Spencer. He dismissed the twelve-year age gap, saying "I just feel you're as young as you think you are." It was while the Queen was riding on her way to trooping the colour that a young man fired six blank shots at her. Also under fire was Prince Andrew, who served on board HMS Invincible as a helicopter pilot during the Falklands war. The US President Ronald Reagan visited the Queen in 1982; a return visit to California was made the next year.

On 29 July 1981 at St. Paul's Cathedral, Prince Charles married Lady Diana; the Archbishop of Canterbury, Dr. Runcie, described the occasion as a fairy-tale. The wedding dress of cream silk with a 25-foot long train was designed by David and Elizabeth Emanuel. Around the world, 750 million television viewers watched. In Britain after the wedding, tea towels (left) were the latest practical souvenir, and the commemorative T-shirt (above) was the latest wearable. It was not long before 'shy Di' emerged from her chrysalis to become a superstar. In her first overseas tour of Australia and New Zealand, she was an instant hit, with the focus of attention on her fashion style. In 1984 'Spitting Image' was first screened: these slippers fitted the mood of the moment.

Commemorative plastic bags were trendy in 1981. Cut-out paper dolls featuring Charles and Di became popular (there had been one in 1953; see p.46), with 'Ch and Di have a baby' appearing in 1982, and m in 1984.

Magazines discovered that a picture of Diana on the cover and, to a lesser extent, Fergie, boosted sales dramatically. Thus during the 1980s Diana mania boomed, and journalists commented on how Diana put fun into royal fashion, or asked "are the royals royal enough?"

Charles and Di's first son, William, was born on 21 June 1982. The Princess of Wales gave birth to her second son, Henry (Harry), on 15 September 1984. Gradually the media were allowed to see more of their family life. By 1986, *Woman's Own* featured 'a look behind the scenes' covering life at Highgrove and, in the following issue, their working life.

The famous kiss landed on the front pages of the tabloid press – and into a movable book. Charles had asked his mother "Is it all right to kiss?" as they stood on the balcony in front of 500,000 onlookers.

On 23 July 1986, the Queen's second son, Prince Andrew, married Sarah Ferguson (referred to by the media as 'Fergie') at Westminster Abbey. Andrew had been created Duke of York just before the ceremony. The couple have two children, Beatrice, born in 1988, and Eugenie, born in 1990. It was in 1992 that Andrew and Fergie separated.

Although watched by a record worldwide audience of 800 million viewers, the selection of souvenirs was limited. A heart-shaped chocolate tin was novel, as was a musical mug that played 'Congratulations' when picked up.

For the marriage of Charles and Diana in 1981, the souvenir industry initially had to rely upon the official photographs taken at the time of their engagement. Of the many poses, there are some eighteen different ones here, as can be seen below. Magazines devised a variety of ways to portray the happy couple. The *Radio Times* took the formal approach, the *TV Times* used a relaxed photograph taken by Patrick Lichfield, and other covers relied on an illustrated interpretation.

Apart from the traditional mugs which were so much part of the souvenir trade, there were others with a little more ingenuity, such as that with Charles's ear as a handle, the mug with a kneeling foot, and a mug illustrated by two primary school children. Rubik's cube was the latest craze, so there was a special royal puzzle edition. The "audio postcard, a revolutionary concept in sound and vision", turned out to be no more than a flimsy record printed on a card of glossy images. For sheer innovation, though, there was no beating the lifelike cardboard Charles and Diana cut-outs that could be fixed to the back door windows of a car, along with the waving hands. You then became 'a royal chauffeur'.

DAILY STAR

COLOUR NEWSPAPER OF THE YEAR

TUESDAY AUGUST 13, 1991

25p

DI-KINI

Holiday Princess takes plunge on love cruise

DIANA the sun goddess looks absolutely Di-lightful in her teeny weeny

---

Daily Mail

THURSDAY, DECEMBER 10, 1992

30p

CHARLES & DIANA
A UNIQUE 24-PAGE ANALYSIS IN WORDS AND PICTURES OF A MARRIAGE THAT CHANGED THE MONARCHY

WITH
- LYNDA LEE-POTTER
- PAUL JOHNSON
- ROBERT LACEY
- WILLIAM REES-MOGG
- NIGEL DEMPSTER
- ANTHONY HOLDEN

END OF THE FAIRYTALE

By RICHARD KAY and GORDON GREIG

AFTER 11 years, the fairytale marriage is over in all but name: Charles and Diana are to separate.

NEWSPAPER OF THE AN

Friday, November 27, 1992   25p   Today's TV: Pages 32 and 33

YOU SPOK

PAGE ONE OPINION
The Queen pays tax and it's a victory for people power...

Pay as you reign ... the Queen's decision to pay income tax could cost her £12million a year

SHE LISTENE

DAILY Mirror

Thursday, December 10, 1992   NEWSPAPER FOR THE NINETIES   27p

INSIDE 12 PAGE ROYAL SOUVENIR

END OF A FAIRYTALE

No kids and no husband - back to an empty house

By JAMES WHITAKER

THE Sun

22p

Monday, October 17, 1994   22p

£500,000 Wheel Of Fortune TONIGHT ITV, 8pm SEE PAGE 7

TV HOST...Carol Smillie

THE CROWN IN CRISIS – SPECIAL EDITION

DIVORCE NOW TO SAVE THE MONARCHY

THE Sun SAYS

IF James Hewitt is a rat for kissing and telling, what does that make Charles?

Major's plea as Charles tells all

NEWS OF THE WORLD

AUGUST 31, 1997   LAST WEEK'S SALE 4,440,692   Price 55p   No.8009

6 am sho issu

DIANA DEAD

Charles told: She died just after 3am

THE FULL TRAGEDY: PAGES 2 and 3

The Mirror

Friday January 29 1999   Historic Edition

337 DAYS TO 2000 AD

TODAY'S PRICE: 0.43 euros / 30p

www.mirror.co.uk

AT LAST!

After 26yrs, Prince Charles shows off his love for Camilla

UNITED: Delighted Charles and lover Camilla drive away from London's Ritz Hotel

FULL STORY PAGES 2, 3, 4 & 5

ROYAL TRIBUTE ISSUE

RadioTimes

LONDON

13–19 September 1997 75p

Diana remembered

Picture: MAX MUMBY

THE TRIBUTE TO DIANA

Diana
THE PEOPLE'S PRINCESS

OK! SPECIAL ISSUE

Every copy bought will help to continue her charitable work

The Nineties

Newspaper headlines summed up the turbu times for the royal far including Princess Dia and Prince Charles's separation in 1992 an divorce in 1995. The tragic death of Diana was a shock to the wh world; she was killed car accident in Paris o 31 August 1997. By 1999, Prince Charles had 'come out' with Camilla Parker Bowle

---

YOU SEXY KING

Birthday boy Charles does a Full Monty

PARTYING: Prince Charles celebrated the eve of his 50th birthday

---

SUN EXCLUSIVE

QUEEN HAS RUBBER DUCK IN HER BATH

By JOHN KAY Chief Reporter

THE Queen shares her royal bath-times with a yellow rubber DUCK, it was revealed yesterday.

it wears a crown!

Thursday, November 29, 2001   30p   www.thesun.co.uk

QUEEN DROPS INTO QUEEN VIC

House of Windsors

NEW SHAME BYERS SPIN D